LET'S PAINT THE '90s!

AN ACTIVITY BOOK WITH PAINT SET AND BRUSH

By Jason Rekulak
Illustrations by Brie Spangler

QUIRK BOOKS

PHILADELPHIA

Library of Congress Cataloging in Publication Number: 2005938982

ISBN-10: 1-59474-107-7
ISBN-13: 978-1-59474-107-4

Printed in China

Typeset in Futura

Designed by Bryn Ashburn
Illustrations by Brie Spangler

Distributed in North America by Chronicle Books
85 Second Street
San Francisco, CA 94105

10 9 8 7 6 5 4 3 2 1

Quirk Books
215 Church Street
Philadelphia, PA 19106
www.quirkbooks.com

Let's Paint Properly!

1 Cover your desk or work surface with newspapers.

2 Remove pictures from the book.

3 Fill a small container (one that will not spill easily) with water.

4 Wet paintbrush, then dip it into the paint.

5 Rinse brush before changing to another color.

6 Let picture dry flat before touching.

* Do not apply paint to clothing, furniture, or other household surfaces. If staining occurs, wash immediately.

* If you have questions, ask Mom or Dad for help!

Let's Paint Roseanne Barr!

Roseanne Barr screeches the National Anthem before a Padres-Reds doubleheader, then ends her performance by grabbing her crotch and spitting on the ground. President George H. W. Bush calls her performance "a disgrace."

July 25, 1990

Let's Paint Vanilla Ice!

Robert Van Winkle (a.k.a. Vanilla Ice) releases his album *To the Extreme*, featuring the hit single "Ice Ice Baby." It sells 15 million copies. (Van Winkle later pays a settlement to Queen and David Bowie for sampling riffs from their song "Under Pressure.")

August 23, 1990

Lousy '90s Movies
Word Search

Listed below are 27 of the worst movies from the '90s. Using these titles as clues, circle the last name of the actor or actress who headlined the film. When you're finished, the remaining letters can be unscrambled to spell a lousy '90s movie starring Matthew Broderick (hint: not *Godzilla* or *Addicted to Love* or *The Road to Wellville*).

```
H I N A N D E R S O N S
T S D A V I S D C P O E
I T E C I S L R P R T V
M R G L E O A C E I A E
S E E A N W S G N N E E
C B N Y F T N E O C K R
O O E O O I B R L E H M
S R R N R E T O L O A Y
T D E P R R G H A R N B
N O S K C A J S T A K S
E D L W I L L I S G S O
R E M L I K N I K L U C
Y H P R U M O O R E E T
```

The Adventures of Ford Fairlane	Ghost Dad	Oscar
Barb Wire	Graffiti Bridge	The Postman
The Bonfire of the Vanities	Holy Man	The Pagemaster
Cool as Ice	Hudson Hawk	Poetic Justice
Cop and a Half	Jack Frost	Ringmaster
Cutthroat Island	Johnny Mnemonic	The Saint
Diabolique	Mary Reilly	Showgirls
Encino Man	Mixed Nuts	Strip Tease
Fair Game	Mr. Wrong	Wild Wild West

Let's Add and Subtract with Milli Vanilli!

After the release of their bestselling album *Girl You Know It's True*, pop duo Fab Morvan and Rob Pilatus won the 1990 Grammy for Best New Artist. They were later stripped of the award when producer Frank Farian revealed that all of Milli Vanilli's songs had been performed by other artists.

November 19, 1990

Let's Paint Teenage Mutant Ninja Turtles!

Donatello, Leonardo, Michelangelo, and Raphael—the four Teenage Mutant Ninja Turtles became Hollywood superstars with the release of their self-titled 1991 film. But two of the turtles on this page are clearly imposters—can you paint the four real reptiles?

Let's Paint Hannibal Lector!

Anthony Hopkins makes his debut as Hannibal Lector in the box office hit, *The Silence of the Lambs*. Connect the dots to ensnare the diabolical Dr. Lector in a straightjacket!

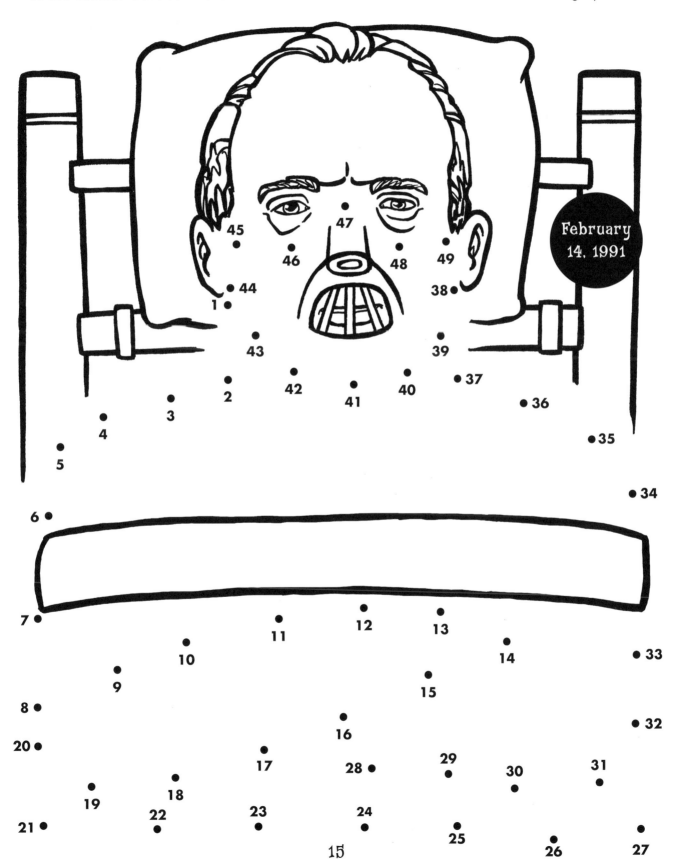

February 14, 1991

Let's Paint *Baywatch*!

Baywatch premieres in syndication after an unsuccessful year on NBC. The hour-long drama becomes the most popular television show in the world, broadcast in more than 120 countries. Producer and star David Hasselhoff shrugs off critics by explaining, "Anyone who makes fun of *Baywatch* is doing it out of ignorance."

September 23, 1991

Let's Paint George H. W. Bush and Kiichi Miyazawa!

While attending a state dinner in Tokyo, President George H. W. Bush vomits into the lap of Japanese Prime Minister Kiichi Miyazawa. Soon afterward, the slang term "Bushusuru" (literally, "to do the Bush thing") enters the Japanese vernacular.

January 8, 1992

Let's Paint Kris Kross!

Thirteen-year-old rappers Chris "Daddy Mack" Smith and Chris "Mack Daddy" Kelly release their first album, *Totally Krossed Out*, which goes on to sell four million copies. The boys were discovered at an Atlanta shopping mall by then-19-year-old producer Jermaine Dupri, who suggested that the duo wear all of their clothing backward.

March 31, 1992

Let's Paint Grunge Rock Stars!

All '90s grunge musicians dressed the same way—but only two of these grunge musicians are dressed *exactly* the same way. Can you find them?

Let's Paint Mayor Marion Barry!

Former Washington, D.C., Mayor Marion Barry is released from prison after serving six months for possession of crack cocaine. To the surprise of many, he goes on to win a city council seat in 1992 and is reelected mayor in 1994.

Let's Paint Aaron Spelling Characters!

TV producer Aaron Spelling created many of the decade's most star-studded television dramas. Paint a line that connects each celebrity with his or her TV show.

Robert Urich

Keri Russell

Carrie-Anne Moss

The Love Boat: The Next Wave
7th Heaven
Melrose Place
Beverly Hills, 90210
Models Inc.
Malibu Shores

Courtney Thorne-Smith

Jason Priestley

Jessica Biel

Let's Paint Arsenio Hall and Bill Clinton!

Presidential candidate Bill Clinton appears on *The Arsenio Hall Show*, dons a pair of black sunglasses, and plays "Heartbreak Hotel" on his saxophone. The appearance is followed by a boost in the polls and an election victory.

June 3, 1992

Let's Paint Vice President J. Danforth Quayle!

At a school spelling bee in Trenton, New Jersey, 12-year-old William Figueroa writes the word "potato" on the chalkboard. Vice President Quayle tells the boy, "You're close, but you left a little something off. The 'e' on the end." Let's help the vice president by painting the missing "e"!

June 15, 1992

potato_

Let's Paint the Olsen Twins!

As *Full House* enters its sixth season, Mary-Kate and Ashley Olsen star in several of their most memorable episodes—including the classic two-parter, "The House Meets the Mouse," in which the entire Tanner clan travels to Disneyland.

September 6, 1992

Let's Paint Billy Ray Cyrus!

Country singer Billy Ray Cyrus releases the hit single "Achy Breaky Heart," and Americans everywhere rediscover the joys of line dancing. It was the first million-selling country single since 1983's "Islands in the Stream" by Kenny Rogers and Dolly Parton.

September 29, 1992

35

Let's Paint Sinéad O'Connor and Pope John Paul II!

Irish rock singer Sinéad O'Connor shocks *Saturday Night Live* audiences by ripping a photograph of Pope John Paul II and crying out, "Fight the real enemy!" Outraged viewers flood the NBC switchboards with 4,484 phone calls.

October 3, 1992

Let's Paint Barney!

In Galveston, Texas, three boys (ages 10, 11, and 12) are fined for assaulting a man in a purple dinosaur suit, in an attempt to remove the head of the costume. A municipal judge scolds the boys for "beating up on a man trying to make an honest living."

October 13, 1993

Let's Paint Nancy Kerrigan and Tonya Harding!

Figure skaters Nancy Kerrigan and Tonya Harding take to the ice in an Olympic skating showdown dubbed "The Battle of Wounded Knee II." (One month earlier, an assailant hired by Harding's ex-husband smashed Kerrigan's knee with a metal baton.) Despite the injury, Kerrigan won a silver medal; Harding placed eighth.

February 25, 1994

O. J. Simpson High-Speed Freeway Maze

Paint a path to safety! Help Al Cowlings steer O. J. and the white Bronco along Interstate 405. Watch out for road blocks, police cars, and news helicopters!

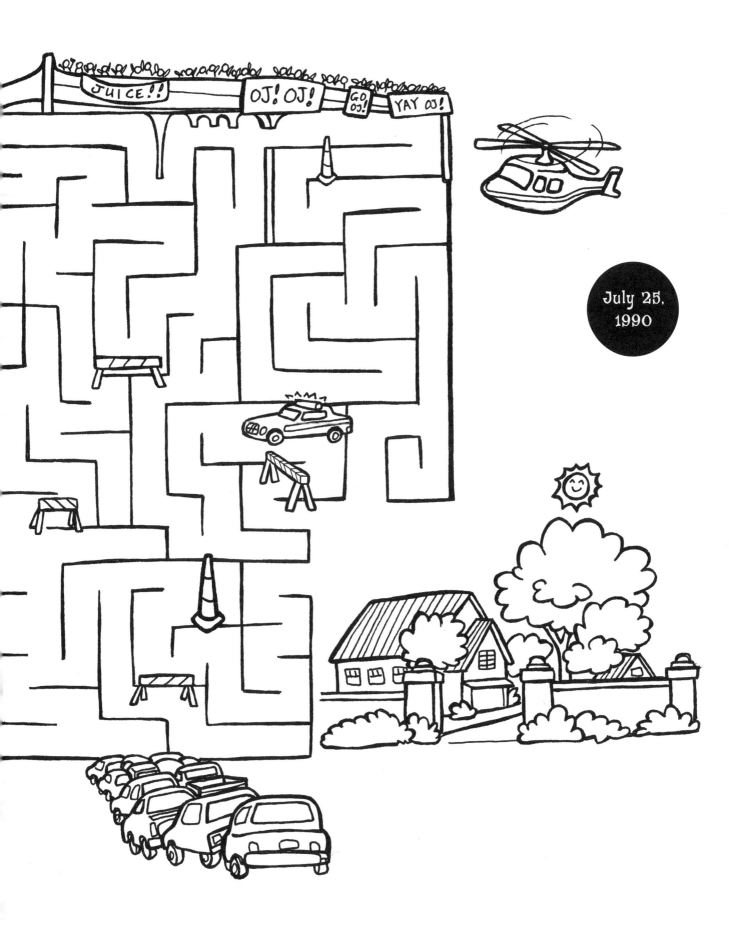

Let's Paint *Pulp Fiction*!

Quentin Tarantino's *Pulp Fiction* opens in the United States, after winning the prestigious Palme d'Or at the Cannes Film Festival. The film is a box office success and inspires dozens of lame knockoffs, including *Go*, *2 Days in the Valley*, and *Eight Heads in a Duffel Bag*.

Let's Paint the Rachel Haircut!

Episode 8 of the NBC sitcom *Friends* introduces the celebrated "Rachel haircut" to audiences across America. Within weeks, hair salons are bombarded with requests for the bouncy layered hairstyle. Let's paint a new look for Jennifer Aniston!

November 10, 1994

Let's Paint Hugh Grant!

British actor Hugh Grant pays $45 to a prostitute named Divine Brown for oral sex. The Los Angeles Police Department sweeps in and arrests both participants. Grant is fined $1080 and later makes numerous high-profile public apologies.

June 27, 1995

BK4454813 062795

LOS ANGELES POLICE

Let's Paint the Cast of *Seinfeld*!

Everyone remembers the time Jerry wore his puffy shirt—but which *Seinfeld* character invented the Urban Sombrero? Who received the Assman license plate? Connect each character with his or her most famous prop(s).

51

Let's Paint Bill Clinton and Monica Lewinsky!

Monica Lewinsky begins a White House internship and later shares an "inappropriate relationship" with President Bill Clinton. Proof of the relationship took the form of a blue dress from the Gap, which was later subpoenaed by Ken Starr.

June 1995

One-Hit Wonder Word Search

The names of 23 popular '90s singles are hidden in this grid. Use the names of the performers to help identify the songs. When you're finished, the remaining 20 letters can be rearranged to spell an additional song and the name of its artists.

```
M O R E T H A N W O R D S A
A N G N I H T D L I W H O C
C E L I R N G I S E H T D H
A O O H E Y J E A L O U S Y
R F E S M B W T Y N N B A B
E U V N R A H E X B R T V R
N S O U O R A V E W O H E E
A H M S F B T L S H L U T A
W T A Y N I I E O A L M O K
I Y T M I E S V O T T P N Y
Y M S L V G L K T S O I I H
A O U A L I O C M U M N G E
T N B E S R V A I P E G H A
S L O T N L E L P H I L T R
E L I S P P O B M M M P S T
```

Ace of Base
Alannah Myles
Aqua
Billy Ray Cyrus
Chumbawamba
Del Amitri
Eagle Eye Cherry
EMF

Extreme
4 Non Blondes
Gin Blossoms
Haddaway
Hanson
Joan Osborne
Len
Lisa Loeb

Los Del Rio
Michael Penn
Naughty by Nature
Right Said Fred
Snow
Tone Loc
Young MC

Let's Paint the Royal Family!

The divorce of Prince Charles and Princess Diana is finalized. From this point on, Diana is no longer called "Her Royal Highness" but rather "Diana, Princess of Wales," a distinction that leaves most Americans hopelessly confused. One year later, the princess was fatally injured in a car accident in Paris.

August 28, 1996

Spice Girl? Dwarf? Or Neither?

So tell me what you want, what you really, really want. Okay: I want you to paint each answer box and indicate whether the name belongs to a Spice Girl, dwarf, or neither.

	SPICE GIRL	DWARF	NEITHER
BABY			
SLEEPY			
IRRITABLE			
SCARY			
HAPPY			
POSH			
SPORTY			
SILLY			
GASSY			
GRUMPY			
GINGER			
DOPEY			
VERNE TROYER			

Let's Paint the Macarena!

Heyyyyyy, Macarena! But wait a second—one of these dancers is *not* doing the Macarena! Can you paint the dancer with the wrong moves?

Let's Paint Cloned Sheep!

Dolly was the first sheep to be successfully cloned, but her scientists made a few mistakes along the way. Can you paint the two sheep that are *exactly* alike?

February
24, 1997

Let's Paint Marshall Applewhite!

Marshall Applewhite leads 38 members of the Heaven's Gate cult to drink a fatal mixture of phenobarbital and vodka. The mass suicide was an attempt to "shed their earthly bodies" and join a spacecraft supposedly traveling behind Comet Hale-Bopp.

March 25, 1997

Let's Paint Mike Tyson and Evander Holyfield!

During the third round of a heavyweight fight in Las Vegas, Nevada, Mike Tyson is disqualified for biting off part of Evander Holyfield's ear. Tyson was fined $3 million and banned from the sport for one year.

June 28, 1997

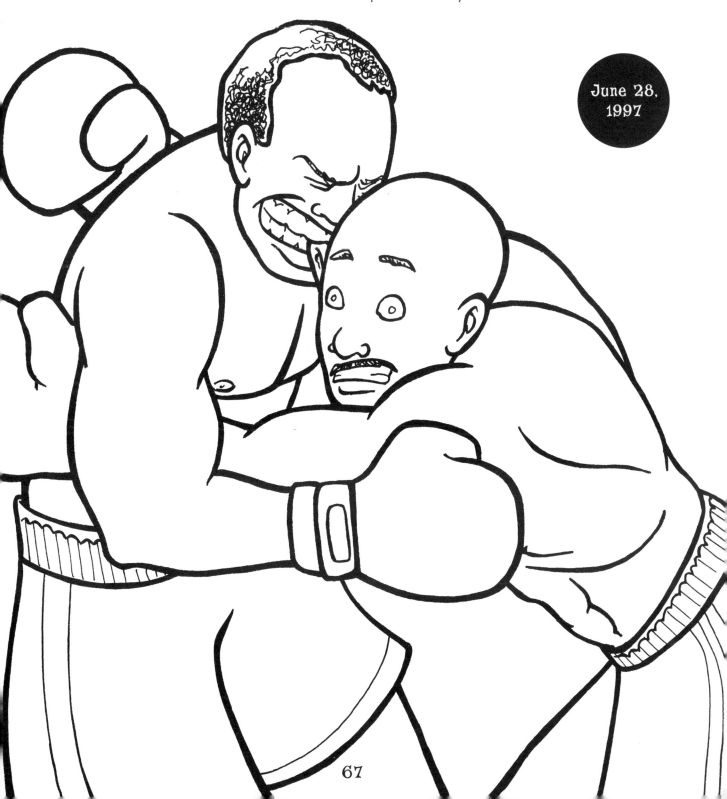

Let's Paint Cameron Diaz!

There's Something About Mary opens in theaters and reaches number one at the box office eight weeks later. It becomes the most successful R-rated comedy of the decade.

July 15, 1997

Let's Paint Dennis Rodman!

Chicago Bulls Power Forward Dennis Rodman appears in a wedding dress to promote his autobiography, *Bad as I Wanna Be*. That same year, he was suspended for 11 games after kicking a cameraman.

August 21, 1996

'90s Bestseller Word Search

The names of 24 bestsellers are listed below. Search for the author's last name in the grid and circle it. When you're finished, the remaining letters will spell the author who had the most bestsellers during the '90s.

```
E F L O W P O W T E R G
D S A C R I C H T O N W
N I Q W A L L E R I Y A
E R E U A K A R K L E L
F R A Z I E R N L E L S
N S S N A V E A T M P C
R R E D F I E L D A I H
E T A L B O M L N H R T
T M D L E F N I E S G U
S T R U O C C M R I R R
E E Y C N A L C E R A O
L R E G N U J M B G Y W
```

A Man in Full
Angela's Ashes
The Bridges of Madison County
The Burden of Proof
The Celestine Prophecy
Cold Mountain
Conversations with God
The Dilbert Principle

Disclosure
Dolores Claiborne
The Firm
The Horse Whisperer
Into Thin Air
Like Water for Chocolate
Men Are from Mars, Women Are from Venus
Midnight in the Garden of Good and Evil

The Perfect Storm
Private Parts
Scarlett
Seinlanguage
Stop the Insanity
The Sum of All Fears
Tuesdays with Morrie
Waiting to Exhale

73

Let's Paint the Guggenheim Museum Bilbao!

The '90s weren't *all* about bad TV shows and celebrity scandals. Frank Gehry's Guggenheim Museum in Bilbao, Spain, was one of the decade's most notable architectural achievements and received accolades from around the world.

October 19, 1997

Let's Paint the Titanic!

Titanic docks in movie theaters, catapulting stars Leonardo DiCaprio and Kate Winslet (as well as director James Cameron and theme song vocalist Celine Dion) to dizzying heights of mega-stardom. It becomes the highest-grossing film in movie history.

December 21, 1997

Let's Paint Woody Allen and Soon Yi Previn!

Sixty-two-year-old filmmaker Woody Allen marries 27-year-old Soon Yi Previn, the adopted step-daughter of Allen's longtime companion, Mia Farrow. (Farrow did not attend the ceremony.)

December 23, 1997

Let's Paint Governor Jesse Ventura!

After careers as a Navy SEAL, professional wrestler, and radio talk show host, Jesse Ventura is elected the 38th governor of Minnesota. He would use his newfound political clout to ask the Dalai Lama if he had ever seen *Caddyshack*.

November 3, 1998

Battle of the '90s Boy Bands!

Connect each of these teen idols with the '90s boy band that made him famous.

Nick Lachey

James Lance Bass

Backstreet Boys
*NSYNC
98 Degrees
Boyz II Men
New Kids on the Block

Jordan Knight

Nick Carter

Nathan Morris

Let's Paint Jerry Falwell and the Teletubbies!

The Reverend Jerry Falwell warns parents that Tinky-Winky, a character on the popular children's show *Teletubbies*, is gay. Falwell notes, "He is purple—the gay-pride color; and his antenna is shaped like a triangle—the gay-pride symbol."

February 9, 1999

Let's Paint Ricky Martin!

Born as Enrique José Martin Morales, this ex-Menudo singer reached the top of the charts with his hit single, "Livin La Vida Loca." It remained in the number one position for five weeks.

May 8, 1999

Elian Gonzalez Ocean Adventure Maze

Miles and miles of ocean separate Elian Gonzalez and Cuba from the coast of south Florida.
Help steer his raft past waves, sharks, and sea monsters—and watch out for Janet Reno!

November 25, 1990

Y2K Codebreaker Challenge

Computer geeks everywhere are warning of a deadly Y2K bug—a computer glitch that threatens to end civilization. Use these video game clues to decipher the secret message—then broadcast it to save the world before it's too late!

Sega Genesis mascot: _____ _____ _____ _____ _____
                                  15   10

Sim City creator (2 words):

_____ _____ _____   _____ _____ _____ _____ _____ _____
 14   6

Id Software's oft-imitated classic: _____ _____ _____ _____
                                   12   13   4

Bestselling PC game of the '90s: _____ _____ _____ _____
                                      20   5

Portable Nintendo player:

_____ _____ _____ _____   _____ _____ _____
 16   2   7

Video game vixen (2 words):

_____ _____ _____ _____   _____ _____ _____ _____ _____
 3   1   8

Trash-talking video game hero (2 words):

_____ _____ _____ _____   _____ _____ _____ _____ _____
    9   19   17   11   18

SECRET MESSAGE:

_____ _____ _____ _____   _____ _____ _____
 1   2   3   4   5   6   7

_____ _____ _____ _____   _____ _____ _____ _____ ,
 8   9   10   11   12   13   14   15

_____ _____ _____ _____ _____ !
 16   17   18   19   20

Let's Paint the Answers!

Lousy '90s Movies Word Search (page 9)

The Adventures of Ford Fairlane—Clay (Andrew Dice)

Barb Wire—Anderson (Pamela)

The Bonfire of the Vanities—Hanks (Tom)

Cool as Ice—Ice (Vanilla)

Cop and a Half—Reynolds (Burt)

Cutthroat Island—Davis (Geena)

Diabolique—Stone (Sharon)

Encino Man—Shore (Pauly)

Fair Game—Crawford (Cindy)

Ghost Dad—Cosby (Bill)

Graffiti Bridge—Prince

Holy Man—Murphy (Eddie)

Hudson Hawk—Willis (Bruce)

Jack Frost—Keaton (Michael)

Johnny Mnemonic—Reeves (Keanu)

Mary Reilly—Roberts (Julia)

Mixed Nuts—Martin (Steve)

Mr. Wrong—Degeneres (Ellen)

Oscar—Stallone (Sylvester)

The Postman—Costner (Kevin)

The Pagemaster—Culkin (Macaulay)

Poetic Justice—Jackson (Janet)

Ringmaster—Springer (Jerry)

The Saint—Kilmer (Val)

Showgirls—Berkley (Elizabeth)

Strip Tease—Moore (Demi)

Wild Wild West—Smith (Will)

The remaining letters spell INSPECTOR GADGET

Let's Paint Teenage Mutant Ninja Turtles! (page 13)

From top left going clockwise, we have an imposter turtle, Donatello, another imposter, Michelangelo, Leonardo, and Raphael.

Let's Paint Hannibal Lector (page 15)

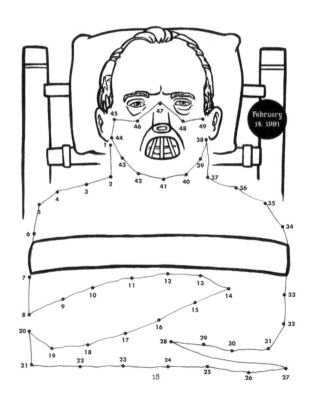

February 14, 1991

92

Let's Paint Grunge Rock Stars!

(page 23)

Let's Paint Aaron Spelling Characters! (page 27)

Robert Urich starred in *The Love Boat: The Next Wave*
Keri Russell starred in *Malibu Shores*
Courtney Thorne-Smith starred on *Melrose Place*
Carrie-Anne Moss starred in *Models Inc.*
Jason Priestley starred in *Beverly Hills, 90210*
Jessica Biel starred in *7th Heaven*

O.J. Simpson High-Speed Freeway Maze

(pages 42–43)

Let's Paint the Cast of *Seinfeld*!

(page 51)

Jerry is paired with the puffy shirt. Kramer is paired with the Assman license plate and the Junior Mints. George is paired with the *Glamour* magazine and the Frogger game. Elaine is paired with the Urban Sombrero.

One-Hit Wonder Word Search (page 55)

Ace of Base—The Sign

Alannah Myles—Black Velvet

Aqua—Barbie Girl

Billy Ray Cyrus—Achy Breaky Heart

Chumbawamba—Tubthumping

Del Amitri—Roll to Me

Eagle Eye Cherry—Save Tonight

EMF—Unbelievable

Extreme—More than Words

4 Non Blondes—What's Up?

Gin Blossoms—Hey Jealousy

Haddaway—What is Love?

Hanson—Mmmbop

Joan Osborne—One of Us

Len—Steal My Sunshine

Lisa Loeb—Stay

Los Del Rio—Macarena

Naughty by Nature—OPP

Right Said Fred—I'm Too Sexy

Snow—Informer

Tone Loc—Wild Thing

Young MC—Bust a Move

The remaining letters spell HOLD ON WILSON PHILLIPS

Spice Girl? Dwarf? Or Neither?

(page 59)

Baby: Spice Girl; Sleepy: Dwarf; Irritable: Neither; Scary: Spice Girl; Happy: Dwarf; Posh: Spice Girl; Sporty: Spice Girl; Silly: Neither; Gassy: Neither; Grumpy: Dwarf; Ginger: Spice Girl; Dopey: Dwarf; Verne Troyer: The diminutive costar of the *Austin Powers* films is neither Spice Girl nor dwarf; he prefers the term "little person."

Let's Paint the Macarena! (page 61)

Dancer #5 has the wrong moves—at no point during the Macarena should you raise your hands over your head.

Let's Paint Cloned Sheep! (page 63)

'90s Bestseller Word Search

(page 73)

A Man in Full—Wolfe (Tom)

Angela's Ashes—McCourt (Frank)

The Bridges of Madison County—Waller (Robert James)

The Burden of Proof— Turow (Scott)

The Celestine Prophecy—Redfield (James)

Cold Mountain—Frazier (Charles)

Conversations with God—Walsch (Neal Donald)

The Dilbert Principle—Adams (Scott)

Disclosure—Crichton (Michael)

Dolores Claiborne—King (Stephen)

The Firm—Grisham (John)

The Horse Whisperer—Evans (Nicholas)

Into Thin Air—Krakauer (Jon)

Like Water for Chocolate—Esquivel (Laura)

Men Are from Mars, Women Are from Venus—Gray (John)

Midnight in the Garden of Good and Evil—Berendt (John)

The Perfect Storm—Junger (Sebastian)

Private Parts—Stern (Howard)

Scarlett—Ripley (Alexandra)

Seinlanguage—Seinfeld (Jerry)

Stop the Insanity—Powter (Susan)

The Sum of All Fears—Clancy (Tom)

Tuesdays with Morrie—Albom (Mitch)

Waiting to Exhale—McMillan (Terry)

The remaining letters spell DANIELLE STEEL

Battle of the '90s Boy Bands!

(page 83)

Nick Lachey—98 Degrees
James Lance Bass—*NSYNC
Nick Carter—Backstreet Boys
Nathan Morris—Boyz II Men
Jordan Knight—New Kids on the Block

Elian Gonzalez Ocean Adventure Maze (pages 88–89)

Y2K Codebreaker Challenge (page 91)

Sega Genesis mascot: Sonic
Sim City creator: Wil Wright
Id Software's oft-imitated classic: Doom
Bestselling PC game of the '90s: Myst
Portable Nintendo Player: Game Boy
Video game vixen: Lara Croft
Trash-talking video game hero: Duke Nukem